Mohamed Akram Arabet

Grading Collocations in Essays

Mohamed Akram Arabet

Grading Collocations in Essays

Noor Publishing

Imprint
Any brand names and product names mentioned in this book are subject to trademark, brand or patent protection and are trademarks or registered trademarks of their respective holders. The use of brand names, product names, common names, trade names, product descriptions etc. even without a particular marking in this work is in no way to be construed to mean that such names may be regarded as unrestricted in respect of trademark and brand protection legislation and could thus be used by anyone.

Cover image: www.ingimage.com

Publisher:
Noor Publishing
is a trademark of
International Book Market Service Ltd., member of OmniScriptum Publishing Group
17 Meldrum Street, Beau Bassin 71504, Mauritius
Printed at: see last page
ISBN: 978-620-0-78094-2

Language Proficiency, Grading, and the Use of Lexical Collocations in Essay Writings by Algerian EFL Learners

Mohamed Akram ARABET, PhD. in Linguistics and Applied Langauges

Email: arabetdoctorat@gmail.com

Abstract

'Pseudo-native speaker' is the term given to a foreign language learner who has reached a high level of proficiency. Such level of proficiency is characterised by the mastery of grammar, vocabulary, and pronunciation. Consequently, a distinction must be drawn between grammatical proficiency and the idiomatic one. Idiomaticity has three basic levels of compositionality: free combinations, collocations, and idioms. The present research work investigates the mastery of Verb+Noun lexical collocations by Algerian EFL learners at Université des Frères Mentouri, Constantine. It is hypothesised that Algerian EFL learners have a low level of mastery in the usage and comprehension of Verb+Noun collocations. It is also hypothesised that the essays of Algerian EFL learners lack the use of appropriate Verb+Noun collocations, a factor that influences the grades they receive. An online corpus (BNC) and two other online websites (Collocation Checker & O.O.C.D) were used as tools to measure learners' collocational competence. Examined collocations were extracted from the learners' examination essays. The analysis was done manually through identification and corpus usage. The findings of the study indicate that Algerian EFL learners have a low competence in dealing with Verb+Noun collocations. They also suggest that Verb+Noun collocational errors that were spotted were not taken into consideration during the correction, even though they are an indispensable part that guarantees the use of correct language. However,

Verb+Noun collocational errors that were spotted did not solely determine the awarded grades. Thus, focus on collocational knowledge is required; teachers must raise their students' awareness on the importance of collocations in improving the oral and written quality of production. Learners have to, deliberately, be able to identify collocations and memorise them within their contexts.

Key Words: Verb+Noun Collocations; Lowest Grades ; Highest Grades; Pseudo-native speaker; Collocational Competence; Essays.

Résumé

'Pseudo-locuteur natif' est un terme accordé à un apprenant d'une langue étrangère qui a attient un haut niveau de maîtrise. Tel niveau de compétence est caractérisé par la maîtrise de la grammaire, le vocabulaire, et la prononciation. Par conséquence, une distinction doit être faite entre la compétence grammaticale et idiomatique. L'idiomaticité a trois niveaux de compositionalité fondamentaux : les combinaisons libres, les collocations, et les idiomes. Cette recherche étudie la maîtrise de collocations lexicales du type Verbe+Nom par les étudiants Algériens à l'université des Frères Mentouri. La premiére hypothése propose que les étudiants Algériens d'Anglais possèdent un niveau de maîtrise bas des collocations lexicales du type Verbe+Nom. La deuxième hypothèse suggère que les essais des étudiants Algériens d'Anglais manquent d'usage approprié des collocations lexicales du type Verbe+Nom, un facteur qui influence les notes qu'ils reçoivent. Un corpus en ligne (B.N.C), et deux autres sites en ligne (collocation checker & O.O.C.D) ont été utilisés comme outils pour mesurer la compétence des collocations par les apprenants. Les collocations examinées ont été extraits des essais des examens faits per les étudiants. L'analyse a été faite manuellement par identification et usage du corpus. Les résultats de l'étude indiquent que les apprenants Algériens de l'Anglais comme langue étrangère ont une maîtrise faible des collocations lexicales du type Verbe+Nom. En outre, les résultats suggèrent que les erreurs faites dans les collocations sous investigation n'ont étaient prises en considération lors de la correction. De plus, les collocations du type Verbe+Nom ne sont pas seuls responsables pour les notes accordées. Donc, la concentration sur la connaissance des collocations est demandée. Les professeurs doivent sensibiliser leurs étudiants sur l'importance des collocations pour améliorer leurs productions orales et écrites. Les apprenants doivent, délibérément, être capables d'identifier les collocations, et les mémoriser dans leurs propres contextes.

Mots Clés: Collocations du Type Verbe+Nom; les Notes les plus Faibles; les Notes les plus Hautes; Pseudo-locuteur natif ; Compétence en Collocations ; les Essais.

Introduction

Inadequate research has been carried out in the area of collocation. Although some researchers have shown interest in collocations, extensive research still needs to be undertaken to highlight its practical importance in improving EFL learners' overall linguistic competence. The topic of collocation raises many questions concerning the measurement of learners' collocational competence, the best methods to teach collocations, or the types of collocations to emphasise on. In order to be able to answer these questions, it is necessary to, first, identify difficulties in mastering collocations (Nesselhauf, 2003). This study, unlike previous studies (Halliday & Hassan 1976; Benson et al. 1986), focuses on Verb + Noun lexical collocations as the mostly used type of collocations. Hatch and Brown (1995) stated that learners acquire collocations in chunks rather than as separate words. The same thing goes to L1 users. In other words, L2 learners learn collocations like infants. The main problem with some studies about collocation is that the definition is vague, no clear and specific definition is given, which makes experimentation difficult (Hussein, 1990;

Farghal & Obiedat, 1995). Firth (1957) defines collocation as the best company a word keeps. Such definition might seem ubiquitous of the notion; however, with closer attention, one would respond by saying that not all words that co-occur are collocations. In Algeria, research on collocation repeatedly tackles its translation (Moussa, 2007; Boussalia, 2010). The present study attempts to shed some light on Algerian EFL learners' knowledge of collocation in essay writing. It investigates the correlation between collocational failure and overall grading in written expression.

1. Literature Review

An essential introduction to the study of language is made by tackling the topic of word knowledge. A distinction is drawn between the three types of word knowledge: knowledge of form, knowledge of meaning, and knowledge of use. These three types make up for the whole study of language. In light of this concept, the notion of collocation can be defined and explained. By understanding what collocations are, one will be able to identify them on the language continuum, and distinguish them from free combinations and idioms.

1.1. Knowing a Word

Human language is made up of words. Words are used for communication. Communication is a human survival mechanism. The only way for a human being to understand language is through the understanding of words. Such an activity can be called 'word knowledge.' However, the difficulty lies in the fact that words cannot be understood on their own as they do not operate in isolation, but, in sequences. In this respect, Nation stated that:

> [w]ords are not isolated components of any given language, but are parts of many joint systems and levels. Consequently, there are many aspects and degrees of word

knowledge required for learners to be able to use words
properly and effectively (as cited in Alsakran, 2011, p. 11).

The levels he talks about are phonological, morphological, syntactic, and semantic. Each system builds up for the previous one, and is indispensable for its existence.

With regard to the four language skills (listening, reading, speaking, and writing), word knowledge can be divided into two spheres: receptive (passive) and productive (active). What is meant by receptive word knowledge is that the learner engages in an input process where he/she simply receives information. Productive word knowledge is the reverse mechanism where the learner reciprocates the knowledge he/she received through an active output embodied in speech and/or writing.

As the term 'word knowledge' can be problematic to the reader, another alternative would be 'vocabulary learning.' Another convention that comes into play is the differentiation between 'breadth' of knowledge and 'depth' of knowledge. The number of words a learner memorises represents the breadth of their knowledge; however, if a learner knows the various aspects of the words he/she memorises, he/she is said to have depth in their word knowledge. The idea of the depth of word knowledge includes the relationships between words, in addition to word associations, collocation, and colligation (as cited in Alsakran, 2011, p. 12).

Word knowledge can be classified into three categories: knowledge of form, knowledge of meaning, and knowledge of use. Each of these categories includes both the receptive and productive aspects. In 'knowledge of form,' spoken forms, written forms, and word parts are treated. Form and meaning, concepts and referents, and associations constitute 'knowledge of meaning.' Finally, in 'knowledge of use,' grammatical functions, collocations, and constraints are taken into consideration (as cited in Alsakran, 2011, pp.12-13). As can be viewed, the categories of word knowledge are interrelated, similar to the common levels of language study (phonology, morphology, syntax, and semantics). Despite the close-identicalness of the two notions (the categories of word knowledge and the levels of language study), the former holds the advantage of investigating word associations –which is pragmatic- since word associations are arbitrary and culturally loaded.

1.2. Definition of Formulaic Language

Opting for a definition of formulaic sequences is no easy task, for they intersect with the many disciplines of language study (grammar, semantics, and pragmatics). According to Wray (2000, p. 464), many attempts were made to categorise formulaic language. Since formulaic language is a learning target for EFL learners, a prior point needs to be clarified; it is of how EFL learners should view it. In this respect, Wood (2009, p. 41) states that:

As long ago as 1983, Pawley and Syder pointed out a link between formulaic language and fluent language use, and that speakers tend to ignore the potentially infinite lexical and grammatical options available. Instead, the norm is to use standard predictable phrases such as 'How are you?' or 'Will you marry me?' rather than grammatical but communicatively unlikely ways of expressing the same meaning or function such as What is your current state of well-being? Or Are you inclined to become my spouse?

Wood (as cited in Kaneyasu, 2012, p. 5) hints at the idea that focusing solely on grammatically constructed sentences will neither result in appropriate usage of that language nor the mastery of it. If a native speaker is exposed to the examples in the quotation, he/she will argue that the expression—will you marry me?—is used in day-to-day conversations instead of —are you inclined to be my spouse? Thus, the first thing to be noted about formulaic language is that it is mostly composed of ready-made phrases that are culturally loaded and are arbitrary, by definition. Dixon and Aikhenvald point out that the idea of 'word' as a basic unit of language was developed for the familiar languages of Europe (Kaneyasu, 2012, p. 5).

Warren (2005, p. 36) says that, according to Mel'cuk, there are more memorised expressions in language than single ones. On the same note, Jackendoff points out to a significant number of phrases that are memorised by speakers of the language. Schmitt and Carter suggest, in agreement, that formulaic sequences take up a hefty portion of spoken language (as cited in Wood, 2009, p. 42).

The prevalence of formulaic language in spoken and written language was measured in order to have a concrete idea on its wide range of existence, hence, its importance. Altenberg recorded a frequency of 80 % of the words in the London-Lund corpus of spoken English which are a part of formulaic sequences. Those words vary from single words to phrases. In a later study, Erman and Warren (as cited in Wood, 2009, p. 42) state that 58.6 % of the corpus investigated in their study was made up of the various types of formulaic sequences. These numbers are considered as a strong evidence of the dominance of formulaic language in language usage. They also prove that they are the most important part of it, because, were they not that paramount, no idioms or collocations would exist in language. Thus, one would not expect to hear 'good morning, good evening' and similar expressions on a daily basis; one would expect novel expressions every day, and society would never be able to agree on communicative patterns that govern their use of language. All this would certainly result in no 'langue.' Similarly, Altenberg claims that up to 80 % of adult native speaker language may be formulaic (as cited in Wray 1999, p. 214).

1.2. The Whole and the Parts

One of the faculties of human cognition is that it tends to store information units that are frequently processed in a specific order for the sake of having faster access to them (Hawkins, as cited in Alhama, 2012, p. 03).

> She would go and smile and be nice and say "So kind of you. I'm so pleased." One is so glad to know people like one's books'. All the stale old things. Rather as you put a hand into a box and took out some useful words already strung together like a necklace of beads (Agatha Christie, as cited in Wray 2002, p. 03).

Breaking a phrase down to single words yields a different meaning from treating it as a whole (Wray, 2002, p. 04). This is the premise behind looking at both, the whole and the parts. Since it is now understood that a formulaic sequence is a fixed phrase that holds its meaning in the associations of words, it is useful to look at it from the inside. One would have a firmer grasp on the concept when he/she looks at the parts in isolation and in combination. It is Wray's extensive research on formulaic language from psycholinguistic, syntactic, and pragmatic points of view that led to this discussion. Hence, the majority of the discussed ideas in this segment are Wray's, unless otherwise cited.

It is worth noting that understanding the processing procedure of retrieving formulaic language is essential to understanding how the speaker/writer uses it in daily life. What is meant by retrieving is the mental procedure of storing the formulaic sequences within the brain, and, then, retrieving them as ready-made chunks for instant use. According to Wray (2002, p. 05), ―words and word strings which appear to be processed without recourse to their lowest level of composition are termed 'formulaic.' This means that, when dealing with formulaic sequences, the brain does not analyse them to their core components—as individual words; they are perceived as holistic expressions. The brain does not seem to have difficulty with formulaic sequences; Ellis reports that ―whether these preferred strings are actually stored and retrieved as a unit or simply constructed preferentially, it has been widely proposed that they are handled effectively like single 'big words' (Wray 2002, p. 05). Sinclair regards them as single choices despite the fact that they seem like segments that can be analysed, they are, in actual fact, single choices (as cited in Wray 2002, p. 07). Research in psycholinguistics reports that language users are sensitive to the frequencies of co-occurrence of numerous word combinations. Hence, the learner's cognitive system is influenced by recurrent usage events and the processing of the component constructions (Ellis, Simpson-Vlach, Maynard, 2008, p. 376).

Looking at formulaic language from a sociolinguistic standpoint yields an insight on the existence and importance of formulaic language in everyday speech. Nattinger and DeCarrico (1992, p, 01) provide this analogy: we, humans, are creatures of habit, not only in our behaviour, but, also, in the language we use. Human behaviour can be categorised in specific patterns of thinking and behaving; these behavioural patterns tend to be shaped by the surrounding environment. Conventions are, then, formed to affirm certain behaviours and reject others. The same thing happens with language: it is a matter of arbitrary convention. Are these phrases fixed? They certainly are. They also hold either positive or negative connotations that are culturally loaded.

―There are words and phrases that we are likely to say when we see a particular friend, or find ourselves in a certain situation‖ (Coulmas, as cited in Wray, 2002, p. 5). This is also apparent in the context of collocation; some words tend to combine well with each other in an expression. Other words, can be formed in a seemingly equally good manner, but, still, sound non-felicitous. This is one side of the coin; there exists another one. One of the main characteristics of language is that it is compositional, i.e. a limited number of sounds can be arranged in arbitrary combinations to, later, make meaningful combinations (Bannard & Matthews, 2008, p. 241).

Fixedness extends that ―the patterning of words and phrases . . . manifests far less variability than could be predicted on the basis of grammar and lexicon alone (Perkins, 1999, pp. 55-56). Compositionality is a core component in understanding formulaicity. It is the degree to which a certain formulaic phrase can be broken down into its components as a method to figure out figurative meaning. Compositionality can be divided into degrees; the less fixed a formulaic expression is, the less compositional it is. In other words, the more likely the expression is to be understood through each core component, the less fixed and compositional it is. Idioms received a considerable amount of attention, because they allow for two interpretations: literal and figurative (Conklin & Schmitt, 2012, p. 47).

1.3. The Relationship between Formulaic and Creative Language

Arguing for the importance and for the prevalent and inherent existence of formulaic language does not entail that creative language is totally discredited. What needs to be done is not to establish balance, since the scientific study of language is no more prescriptive. Rather, a line needs to be drawn between compositional and non-compositional principles. It can be said that:

Early criticism of generative syntactic theory for failing satisfactorily to accommodate idioms (e.g. Chafe, 1968; Weinreich, 1969; Fraser, 1970; Makkai, 1972; Bolinger, 1976; Coulmas, 1979; Gazdar et al., 1985) has led to the admission of irreducible formulas to the lexicon. Thus, the formulaic sequences which are syntactically irregular or semantically opaque achieve the status of 'big words' (Ellis, 1996, p. 111).

This is where Chomsky's theory fell short, by marginalising the role of formulaic language and promoting basic grammatical construction as the sole mechanism to language study. The aim here is to establish a balance between the two forms.

Formulaic sequences which are of a regular construction are excluded, for the lexicon cannot contain any items with a regular internal structure. Rather, all sequences of words, and indeed of morphemes, which can be assembled by rule, must be assembled by rule (Wray & Perkins, 2000, p. 10).

What ensues out of such view is problematic. Consider these examples: *I am really glad to see you/ I am in a very glad state after seeing you/Seeing you has brought me real gladness.* According to native speakers, the last two forms would be considered odd despite their grammaticality.

The solution lies:

> In recognising a central role for formulaic sequences, and
> allowing for their presence in the lexicon, it is not
> necessary to deny our capability for creativity, only to
> relegate it from the position of sole strategy (Wray, 1992,
> pp. 17f). Such a model of dual processing is one way of
> accommodating the holistic and analytic features of
> language (Wray & Perkins, 2000, p. 11).

Wray goes on to state that establishing a balance between novel and ready-made phrases is useful for communicative language. The creative process allows for freedom in encoding and decoding. On the other hand, the holistic system guarantees economy of effort when dealing with familiar expressions (Wray, as cited in Wray & Perkins, 2000, p. 11). The view of language differs between linguists and language learners, in this respect. The former see it as an analytical system that is based on rules; the latter see it as a memory system that is based on prefabricated chunks (Skehan, as cited in Okuwaki, 2012, p. 5). Wray and Perkins (2000) conclude by stating:

> Without the rule-based system, language would be limited
> in repertoire, clichéd, and, whilst suitable for certain types
> of interaction, lacking imagination and novelty. In contrast,
> with only a rule-based system, language would sound
> pedantic, unidiomatic and pedestrian. It would require full

access to all of the language faculties at all times and there
would be no `shortcuts'. It would be a much more accurate
reflection of what Chomsky terms competence, but not a
reflection of communicative competence (Wray & Perkins,
2000, p. 10).

1.4. Definition of Collocation

Collocations have been recognised to distinguish a native speaker from a
foreign language learner. Usually, one way a non-native speaker may offer help
is by saying 'Can I help you?' Meanwhile a native speaker would say 'Can I
give you a hand?' (Salkauskiene, 2002, as cited in Farrokh, 2012, p. 56).
Although a non- native speaker might succeed syntactically, he/she may not
sound a native-like in terms of which words combine with which. English,
similar to many languages, has its own share of re-occurring word combinations.
These word combinations arbitrarily co-occur. A native speaker says 'ultimate
goal' and not 'last goal'; one 'pays a visit', but does not 'make a visit' (Farrokh,
2012, p. 56). Prodromou (2004, as cited in Farrokh, 2012, p. 56) says:

knowing the meaning of a word not only requires knowing its

dictionary definition; one must also know the type of words

with which it is often associated. Collocations, either fixed or

more flexible, are the result of many years of habitual use by

fluent speakers of the English.

Palmer (1933) introduced the notion of collocation. According to him, it is
"a string of words that must or should be learned, or is best or most conveniently
learnt as an integral whole or independent entity, rather than by the process of

piecing together their component parts" (Ganji, 2012, p. 125). Firth (1957) followed later, and was recognized as the one who introduced this concept to the world.

During the last decades, research in linguistics has given much importance to collocation. Scholars, teachers, and corpus designers understood its importance during the language learning process. They mentioned that the increase in linguistic competence is primary in the enhancement of learners' communicative competence, and the approximation to native-like fluency (Darvishi, 2011, p. 52). On the same note, teachers' ability to identify collocational errors to EFL leaners can significantly increase their awareness of the subject. Therefore, studying miscollocations is equally important to studying correct ones, for it helps instructors to focus on the difficult ones (Darvishi, 2011, p. 52-53).

Focus on collocation by many scholars led to a variety of definitions. For Firth (1957, p. 179, as cited in Salman and Mansoor, 2013, p. 04) "you shall know a word by the company it keeps." According to Lewis (1997, p.44, as cited in Farrokh, 2012, p. 57) "collocations are those combinations of words which occur naturally with greater than random frequency. Collocations co-occur, but not all words which co-occur, are collocations." This states clearly that collocations have their specific characteristics which distinguish them from other word combinations like free combinations and idioms. Hardi (2008) defines collocation as words frequently recurring in a text. This co-occurrence, he believes, is frequent enough to make a pair of words as a collocational phrase. Hardi's words denote the characteristic of frequency which is primary to identifying collocations. However, frequency hits which qualify a certain word combination to move from free combination to collocation differ according to scholars and corpora. Some scholars set the bar to 40 hits per 100 million words; others suggest the hits should reach 50 hits per 100 million words.

1.5. Collocational Competence

As much as grammatical competence is important to reach native-like proficiency, collocational competence makes a foreign language learner a pseudo-native speaker. There are many advantages that collocational competence offers. According to Henriksen (2013), collocational competence helps:

> 1) to make idiomatic choices and come across as native-like; 2) to process language fluently under real-time conditions (Columbus, 2010; Ellis et al., 2008); 3) to establish 'islands of reliability' (Dechert, 1983; Raupach, 1984) which enable the language user to channel cognitive energy into more creative production; 4) to disambiguate meaning of polysemous words, e.g. the verb *commit* in the following collocational contexts: *commit a crime, commit oneself, commit to memory*; and 5) to understand connotational meaning (what Sinclair, 2004 has described as semantic prosody), e.g. the fact that the verb *cause* is often associated with negative connotations as in *cause an accident.* (p. 33)

In other words, appropriate understanding of collocations allows the reader or listener to achieve communicative competence.

1.6. Types of Collocations

The various perspectives the notion of collocation was viewed from led to a different categorisation. According to Chia-Chuan, "Cowie and Mackin (1973) classified idioms and collocations into four categories based on idiomaticity from most to least fixed: pure idioms, figurative idioms, restricted collocations, and open collocations (2005, p. 11). On a different note, Wood (as cited in Darvishi, 2011, p. 53) categorised collocations into idioms, colligations, and free combinations. His categorisation was based on semantic and syntactic criteria. For Lewis (1997), collocations were classified into strong, weak, frequent, and infrequent (Darvishi, 2011, p. 53). The categorisation adopted in this research is developed by Bahns. According to Boussalia (2010, p. 15), collocations can be classified into two main categories: grammatical collocations and lexical collocations.

Grammatical collocations contain prepositions, sometimes occurring with verbs, nouns, or adjectives, e.g. (*reach down, put forth*), (by *car, on foot*), or (*interested in, happy with*) (McKeown & Radev, p. 05). Bahns (1993, p. 57, as cited in Boussalia 2010, p. 15) notes that they "(usually) consist of a noun, an adjective or a verb, plus a preposition or a grammatical structure such as an infinitive or clause."

On the other hand, lexical collocations are "restricted lexically" (McKeown & Radev, p. 05-06). Benson (1985, p. 62) explains that "lexical collocations contain no subordinate element; they consist of two lexical components" (Boussalia 2010, p. 15-16). This means that there are no grammatical components within the word combination, only lexical ones (content words). According to Gabrielatos (1994, p. 02):

there are three factors determining the categorising of a lexical collocation: the degree of probability that the items will co-occur, the degree of fixity of the combination (i.e. grammatical restrictions), and the degree to which the meaning of the combination can be derived from its constituent parts.

There are six types of lexical collocations:

1.	Verb + noun: pay a visit.

2.	Adjective + noun: heavy rain.

3.	Noun + verb: the cat cuddles.

4.	Adjective + adjective: closely related.

5.	Verb + adverb: announce happily.

6.	Adverb + adjective: totally bewitched (Bahns, 1993, p. 57).

2. The Study

The present work investigates the use of Verb+Noun lexical collocations in the essays of Algerian second year undergraduate EFL learners at the department of English at Université des Frères Mentouri, Constantine. It is to discuss the following questions:

1.	To what extent do second year EFL undergraduate students of English at Université des Frères Mentouri, Constantine master the use of Verb+Noun collocational language while writing essays?

2.   To what extent do the Verb+Noun collocational errors influence the grades received by second year Algerian EFL undergraduate students of English at Université des Frères Mentouri, Constantine?

It is hypothesised that:

1.   Algerian EFL second year undergraduate students of English at Université des Frères Mentouri, Constantine 1, have a low level of mastery in the usage and comprehension of V+N collocations.

2.   The essays of Algerian EFL second year undergraduate students of English at Université des Frères Mentouri, Constantine lack the use of appropriate collocations, which influences the grades they receive.

3.   The grades Algerian EFL second year undergraduate students at the University of Mentouri Brothers, Constantine 1 have received are influenced by the lack of use of the V + N appropriate collocations.

2.1. Data Gathering Tools

The study used three research tools: Collocation checker, Oxford Online Collocation Dictionary (O.O.C.D), and the British National Corpus (BNC).

Collocation checker is an online software, which permits the researcher to identify correct and erroneous collocations. It shares the same database of BNC. All word combinations retrieved from students' essays were analysed via this software.

The second tool is O.O.C.D, which is an online software, too. It provides all the possible collocational hits for the searched word, in addition to examples retrieved from the BNC. Its main function -in this study- is to distinguish collocations from free combinations.

The British National Corpus is the third tool. It is an online corpus that comprises 100 million words. BNC contains authentic data, and is considered as a reliable source for examining collocation. A high-frequency hit in BNC is proof of a well-combined word combination. Examples are provided in Table 01. The basic threshold in this study is 40 hits per word combination. All collocations which did not score 40 hits were considered as free combinations, instead.

2.2. Research Method

The present section describes the research method applied in the study. It contains the frequent examples, the main criteria for selecting collocations, and the method of application of the research tools.

Pattern	Correct Collocation	Erroneous Collocation	Suggestion for Improvement
V+N	attend classes do homework answer a question	stare star promote appetite do preparation pay time	watch star increase appetite make preparation spend time

Table 01: Typical V+N Collocation Type Found in this Study

The study was based on three criteria to identify acceptable collocations and erroneous ones. Table 02 illustrates these criteria.

Criterion 01	The sense of the verb is so specific that it can only combine with a small set of nouns.
Criterion 02	The verb in this sense cannot be replaced by their syntactically and semantically possible choices.
Criterion 03	Word combinations which have high frequency hits in the British National Corpus are considered as well-formed collocations (40 hits).

Table 02: Criteria for Choosing Collocations in this Study

The initial two criteria are flexible; however, the third one is fixed. In other words, the verb is considered to be 'restricted' if one or both of the restrictedness and substitutability criteria were met. Nonetheless, the combination has to score, at least, 40 hits.

A primary task was to identify erroneous collocations. The three research tools were used in the aforementioned order.

Collocation checker was used to spot wrong collocations. After a word combination is inputted, collocation checker indicates whether the combination is correct or erroneous. However, that does not entail that all acceptable word combinations –according to collocation checker-are collocations. After identifying wrong collocations, the send task was to distinguish free combinations from collocations.

O.O.C.D was used to determine whether the verb + noun investigated collocate or not.

BNC came as a final step to ensure that word combinations labelled as 'collocations' by O.O.C.D thoroughly fulfil the third criterion, high frequency of co-occurrence. If a combination were labelled as a 'collocation' by O.O.C.D, but did not score, at least, 40 hits in BNC, it would be classified as a free combination.

The efficacy of using all of the three online tools is that they share the same database, which ensures congruence in results.

2.3. Population and Sample

The sample of the study consists of second year EFL students at the University of 'Frères Mentouri' (Constantine, Algeria). These students have been studying English for nine years. They studied written expression for 3 sessions a week, which is an equivalent of 4.5 hours for the last 2 years. The samples analysed in the study are students' essays that were written during the second semester examinations. The reason behind the selection of examinations' essays is to ensure seriousness in production since these essays were rated by written expression teachers. The topics were mainly social ones: gifts received in the past, students' dream house, and the consequences of moving out of one's native town. Such topics are common to students, and they, presumably, possess the appropriate vocabulary and ideas to elaborate on them. 66 randomly-selected essays were analysed, which is fifth of the total number of students. It is worthy to mention that the examples reported from students' essays were copied with all the mistakes.

2.4. Results and Discussion

The study recorded 616 word combinations (free combinations, collocations, and idioms). In table 03, proportionate numbers of each category are represented.

Total	Free Combinations	Collocations	Idioms
616 (100%)	379 (61.53%)	237 (38.47%)	0 (0%)

Table 03: Total Number of Word Combinations in Students' Compositions

It is predictable that learners use free combinations more than collocations, and that idioms will be of a lesser use. The reason is that collocations and idioms are context-bound and of arbitrary use. What is noticeable is that in 66 essays written by the students, no idiom was identified. This could be due students' ignorance of idioms as essential in improving the quality of writing.

237 collocations were found in students' compositions. Only 38.82 % of them were correct. Table 04 illustrates the findings.

Composition	Acceptable Collocations	Unacceptable Collocations
	92 (38.82 %)	145 (61.18 %)

Table 04: Frequency of Acceptable/Unacceptable Collocations in Students' Compositions

The high percentage of erroneous collocations shows clearly that second year EFL learners at Frères Mentouri university lack collocational competence. Although students were given freedom to choose topics to write about, they were unsuccessful in using the appropriate V+N combinations -based on the context of writing. These results open speculation on students' ability to use the most common type of lexical collocations (V+N) if writing topics were more difficult and more science-based.

The following section focuses on the essays with the lowest grades. It attempts to examine the influence of V+N collocational errors on the grades. It also investigates written expression teachers' awareness of collocations during the correction. In this sense, it considers 06 copies that were awarded the lowest grades.

The Compositions with the Lowest Grades:

Copy Number 01:

Grade	Number of Acceptable Collocations	Number of Unacceptable Collocations
07.5	01	04

Table 05: Frequency of Acceptable/Unacceptable V+N Collocations in Copy 01

The only case where the V+N collocation was correctly used was in this example:

- Moving to a new town puts you in a situation where you must *to have a good and strong control* your self to have a nice life.

Compared to the other 04 unacceptable V+N collocations, it is obvious that the learner has a low level of mastery of Verb+Noun collocations. What needs to be stressed, though, is the grade. Taking into consideration the importance of V+N collocations among other types of lexical/grammatical collocations, the teacher, in this case, was accurate to reward 7.5 as a grade.

Copy Number 02:

In the second copy, there were 04 V+N free combinations. What was unexpected is the low number of erroneous collocations, because, regarding the final grade, it can be assumed that either the learner ignored other important techniques of essay writing, or the teacher did not consider the fact that he/she made few a few collocational errors.

Grade	Number of Acceptable Collocations	Number of Unacceptable Collocations
08	04	02

Table 06: Frequency of Acceptable/Unacceptable V+N Collocations in Copy 02

In essay writings, it is usually expected that free combinations are used more than collocations, especially for EFL learners. However, using collocations more than free combinations is not a sign that there is a lack of use in the latter. What is more important is the frequency of collocational error in the essays; the less collocational errors a learner makes, the better the grading should be.

Some of the instances where free combinations were used include the following:

1. For me, I like *to give gifts*, because I feel that is the most thing that makes people so happy, and you can sometimes achieve their dream.

2. First of all, computure is a wonderful gift. I like *to receive computure* [unclear word] the one who I like so much especially if he secceed in his study.

Copy Number 03:

In this copy, the number of V+N acceptable collocations surpassed that of unacceptable ones. What is obvious is that the student did not receive 08/15, because he/she failed to adhere to the writing techniques (introduction, body, conclusion, punctuation, etc.). Although V+N free combinations were not used intensely, it must be noted that that did not influence the gist of the essay.

Grade	Number of Acceptable Collocations	Number of Unacceptable Collocations
08	04	01

Table 07: Frequency of Acceptable/Unacceptable V+N Collocations in Copy 03

The mistake that was made in the recorded unacceptable V+N collocation was the absence of the preposition "in". The example is phrased in the following way:

- Moving from one place to another sometimes creates social problems such as lake of communication. They find lot of difficulties to contact with the other's and they find them selvs which *results some illnesses* for them as phobia xenophobia or a fear of being amoung people.

Copy Number 04:

For the other word combinations, there were 04 correct Verb+Noun collocations, and only 02 erroneous ones. The essay, however, received a grade 07/15. Such grade might be considered not enough for a student who only made 02 mistakes in Verb+Noun collocations. Nonetheless, there were other factors coming into play when the paper was corrected.

Grade	Number of Acceptable Collocations	Number of Unacceptable Collocations
07	04	02

Table 08: Frequency of Acceptable/Unacceptable V+N Collocations in Copy 04

Analysing copy 04 carefully, one would highlight the following mistakes:

1. Difficulty in using the appropriate tense

2. Numerous mistakes in punctuation.

3. Absence or inappropriateness of the thesis statement.

4. Lack of parallelism within sentences.

5. An insufficient development of the essay, in general.

Although all these problems contributed in the degeneration of the quality of the essay, what is noticed in copy 04 (as well as other copies) is that the teachers did not signal the collocational errors of the learners. This could be due to the significant number of copies to correct; however, skipping such mistakes shows that the teachers were not aware of these mistakes.

The mistakes that were constantly highlighted were spelling, tense, and, sometimes, punctuation mistakes. Such finding provokes speculation about the teachers' attitude toward collocational knowledge and collocational competence.

The most justifiable interpretation is that teachers are not aware of the importance of collocations in writing.

Copy Number 05:

Copy 05 has the highest number of acceptable collocations among all the lowest grades' copies, and with only one erroneous collocation. Although there were no Verb+Noun free combinations in the whole essay, that did not affect the message delivery.

Similar to the other copies, the teacher did not highlight any of the collocational errors made in the essay –including V+N collocations. Copy 05 contained some grammatical mistakes:

1. Articles

2. Tense

3. Prepositions

There were also spelling and punctuation mistakes.

Grade	Number of Acceptable Collocations	Number of Unacceptable Collocations
06.5	06	01

Table 09: Frequency of Acceptable/Unacceptable V+N Collocations in Copy 05

The essay composed in copy 05 was cluttered with many mistakes the affected the negatively. The fact that it received a mark of 6.5/15 is acceptable. In other words, even though the collocational success frequency was high, that did not help in increasing the mark. Such result is acceptable since writing is an interconnected organism of various elements and techniques, carefully interwoven to produce a solid composition.

Copy Number 06:

Copy 06 received the lowest grade amongst all the lowest grades' copies. What is contradictory about this copy is that no unacceptable V+N collocation was recorded. Since this last section focuses mainly on errors –as well as other aspects- and their influence on the grading of learners' compositions, what resulted in such a low grade is the shortness of the essay. Even the teacher commented "is this an essay???" The essay recorded:

1. Absence of thesis statement

2. Spelling mistakes

3. Insufficient development of ideas

4. Punctuation mistakes

Since there were no erroneous collocations in the study, it is obvious that the aforementioned remarks led to the low copy 05 received.

Grade	Number of Acceptable Collocations	Number of Unacceptable Collocations
05	05	00

Table 10: Frequency of Acceptable/Unacceptable V+N Collocations in Copy 06

The following are some of the cases of acceptable collocations in copy 06:

1. Some parents are so strict with their children. First, parents have a big responsibility which is *protecting their children* a maximum because parents have more experience than them.

2. Some parents are so strict with their children. First, parents have a big responsibility which is protecting their children a maximum because parents *have more experience* than them.

The following section takes into account the copies that were awarded the highest grades.

Copies with the Highest Grades

Copy Number 01:

Number of Free Combinations	Number of Collocations	Number of Idioms
00	01	00

Table 05: Number of Free Combinations/ V+N Collocations/ Idioms in Copy Number 01

With regard to Copy Number 01, there are no significant errors that ought to be mentioned, except for very few grammatical mistakes, such as the article in one case, or spelling mistakes ("responsability" instead of "responsibility"). Therefore, when such mistakes are almost non-existent, the teacher could have turned to the erroneous V+N collocations. However, those mistakes were not taken into consideration. This, again, confirms what has been stated before, that teachers pay no attention to collocational errors in the essays of their students due to a lack of awareness of their importance and existence or, probably, because they had not taught them during the academic year.

It is common amongst people who are constantly exposed to English that it is not appropriate to say "to put the rules" instead of "to make/to establish the rules."

It can be said, hence, that, at least, in Copy Number 01, the teacher did not take into consideration collocations when awarding the grade.

In Copy Number 01, there were 03 cases of acceptable V+N collocations:

1. Parents want *to protect their children* from negative things such as drugs. Always, they feel afraid about their future, they want it to be a better one.

2. The second cause that *makes parents* so strict is responsibility, it is not easy to take a good care of their children.

3. Even if they are so strict they look for something beneficial, we must respect them and *follow their rules*.

Copy Number 02

The mistakes that were collected in Copy number 02 can be summarised in the following points:

1. Spelling errors

2. Tense errors

On one hand, the thesis statement was well-phrased, and the ideas were, to a certain extent, adequately developed. On the other hand, from a collocational standpoint, the teacher gave no importance to the V+N erroneous collocation in the essay.

Number of Free Combinations	Number of Collocations	Number of Idioms
05	04	00

Table 06: Number of Free Combinations/ V+N Collocations/ Idioms in Copy Number 02

The following are some of the instances of the acceptable collocations in Copy Number 02

1. In this respect, families who choose to change their origin town may *face many problems* related to their children and their social life.

2. Rather, they are a result of a long run relationships. We *build our relationships* with our parents, brothers, sisters, friends and with customers in our business over a long spun of experiences and transactions. So, to move to a new town means to lose some of the social relationships.

Copy Number 03

The case of Copy number 03 is a confirmation that the teachers are not aware of the restricted relations between words—Verb+Noun in this case or, again, sufficed on correcting what they have taught. How come that a students' copy, which contains 08 erroneous Verb+Noun collocations be awarded 16? The answer is that, while correcting the paper, the teacher did not consider the notion of collocation as crucial in essay writing. It also shows that the teachers are not aware of the difference between "having a scholarship" and "winning a scholarship." This trend has been recurrently noted and highlighted throughout the practical side of the thesis.

Number of Free Combinations	Number of Collocations	Number of Idioms
01	04	00

Table 07: Number of Free Combinations/ V+N Collocations/ Idioms in Copy Number 03

The essay contained almost no spelling or tense errors; the thesis statement was well-phrased. All these factors led the teacher to award such a good mark, neglecting the essence of many of the sentences, that is the verb and the noun that combines with it.

The acceptable collocations in Copy number 03 are stated as follows:

1. I am of course aware of the fact that every single human being is interested in a particular and certain sort of things he would like *to have as a gift*.

2. He is an engineer in architecture who *owns his private successful company*.

3. This scholarship may be a basic thing in advanced nations, but it is life saving to us, and more particularly, me. It would *provide me with opportunities* I have never dreamt of encountering.

Copy Number 04

The use of Verb+Noun word combinations—especially free combinations—was prevalent in Copy Number 04, the total of 17 word combinations (09 V+N free combinations/ 08 V+N collocations). In addition, 07 unacceptable collocations were found in Copy Number 04.

What is expectedly similar to the previous copies is that the teacher ignored all of the 07 unacceptable collocations, the equivalent of 46.67 %, and awarded the essay a mark of 14/15. Even on the student's examination paper, there were no corrections concerning the unacceptable collocations.

Number of Free Combinations	Number of Collocations	Number of Idioms
01	04	00

Table 08: Number of Free Combinations/ V+N Collocations/ Idioms in Copy Number 04

It has to be noted that the thesis statement in Copy Number 04 was successful in terms of topic and subtopics; parallelism was achieved, in addition to appropriate punctuation. Although there were some minute blemishes in punctuation, the procedure of writing the essay in Copy Number 04 was successful, to a great extent. Nevertheless, adhering to the various essay writing techniques does not entail a total negligence of Verb+Noun collocations as major factors in determining the quality.

It is compulsory to ask this question: What is the use of successfully implementing all the writing techniques if the core of the sentences that make up the essay is unacceptable? It goes without saying that the answer is that it is useless. Another way to put it is to ask: Does the EFL student learn syntax and semantics first, or writing techniques? The answer is obviously that syntax and semantics are more important to learn, because they come before writing during the process of language learning.

Some of the acceptable collocations that were found in Copy number 04 are:

1. Every father does his best to save his child, so it is obvious that he will try anything in order to achieve his desire, and being so strict is one of the aspects that the fathers or mothers should follow and every parent has his own reasons about why he should be so strict.

2. Every father does his best to save his child, so it is obvious that he will try anything in order to achieve his desire, and being so strict is one of the aspects that the fathers or mothers should follow and every parent has his own reasons about why he should be so strict.

Copy Number 05

In Copy number 05, there were 07 Verb+Noun free combinations, 02 acceptable Verb+Noun collocations, and only 01 unacceptable Verb+Noun collocation.

There were some spelling mistakes in Copy Number 05. Other than that, the thesis statement was acceptable, with clear subtopics. It was also concise and precise. The use of tense was successful throughout the essay. Therefore, with regard to the sole V+N collocational error in the whole essay, the awarded grade was deserved. However, the teacher showed, again, unawareness or neglect toward the collocational mistake that had been made.

Number of Free Combinations	Number of Collocations	Number of Idioms
00	06	00

Table 09: Number of Free Combinations/ V+N Collocations/ Idioms in Copy Number 05

The two acceptable collocations in Copy Number 05 are the following:

1. In our continuous pursuit of happiness, we may travel *to achieve that goal*.

2. In our continuous pursuit of happiness, we may travel to achieve that goal; we may *leave our homes* to seek for a new life in a new town.

It needs to be noted that they were copied exactly in the same way they were written in the essays.

Copy Number 06

The number of V+N unacceptable collocations in Copy Number 06 is 04; that is the equivalent of 40 % of all the V+N collocations. Nonetheless, the essay received 16, a mark only given to outstanding compositions. For a composition to be labelled as "outstanding", it has to be devoid of errors, mainly syntactic and semantic. So, how come that an essay containing 04 unacceptable V+N collocations receive such a high grade? The answer is because the teacher did not take into consideration collocational knowledge as a key component in language.

Number of Free Combinations	Number of Collocations	Number of Idioms
03	05	00

Table 10: Number of Free Combinations/ V+N Collocations/ Idioms in Copy Number 06

Starting with the thesis statement, although it fulfilled the requirements of a good one, two collocational errors were spotted in that sentence. Written Expression of undergraduate second year instruct their students on how to write an appropriate thesis statement. Therefore, when correcting students' examination papers, they give more importance to the latter than other aspects of writing. In the case of Copy Number 06, the teacher did not correct the inappropriately combined verbs and nouns. This can be deduced due to the fact that they have not written any remarks, nor have they crossed or highlighted any of the inappropriate V + N collocations.

For the acceptable V+N collocations in Copy Number 06, here are some of them:

1. *Having an amazing car* as a gift would be a great thing.

2. I would take it every night, go to the highway, and drive as fast as I can. But I would never *drive it (the car)* in town because I do not want someone to crash it.

To conclude this section, it is crucial to mention that the use of erroneous collocations is by no means the sole factor that contributed to the poor quality of the learners' essays. And it is also not taken as the only variable of evaluation.

Nevertheless, it is clear, thus far, that the use of erroneous collocations—V+N—significantly lowers the quality of the written production, regardless whether the Written Expression teacher takes into account the appropriate use of collocations while correcting or not. It has to be understood that formulaic language—collocations included—makes up 80 % of the language repertoire. Hence, it is undeniably to be equally taken into consideration, even if it is not taught by the Written Expression teacher, similar to grammar.

Conclusion

This paper sketched the collocational status quo of the Algerian second year EFL learners at Université des Frères Mentouri, Constantine. It has confirmed the hypothesis that Algerian EFL learners have a low level of mastery of Verb + Noun lexical collocations. As a whole, it is to be concluded that considering all word combinations as collocations is incorrect. It is now admitted that identifying collocations from other word combinations is difficult due to their vague nature that falls between free combinations and idioms. The study stated that in order to be able to classify a given word combination as collocation, three criteria—or at least two—need to be met: restricted sense, restricted substitutability, and high frequency of co-occurrence. The obtained results show the indispensability of collocational competence in achieving efficiency in essay writing, therefore, language proficiency. The majority of the essays which contained numerous mistakes were graded from average to low. The essays with the lowest grades did not necessarily contain the highest frequency of unacceptable V+N collocations, a result indicating that collocational errors were not taken into consideration when putting grades. This shows that written expression teachers are unaware of the importance of collocations in determining the writing quality. Therefore, the study encourages teachers and instructors to give more importance to teaching collocations as an inseparable factor to becoming a pseudo-native speaker. Moreover, they are encouraged to take collocations into consideration when correcting students' essays. In addition to that, not only do learners need to be exposed to correct collocations, but, to erroneous ones, too. This is because the trial-error mechanism used by L2 learners cannot be applied to ready-made chunks. To sum it up, it is necessary to carry out further research in this field of study through the investigation of other types of collocations.

References

Alhama, R. G. (2012). The formulaicity of language: a computational proposal to detect linguistic constructions. Unpublished master thesis, University of Barcelona, Spain.

Alsakran, R. A. (2011). The productive and receptive knowledge of collocations by advanced Arabic-speaking ESL/EFL learners. Unpublished master dissertation, Colorado State University, The United States of America.

Bannard, C., Matthews, D. (2008). Stored word sequences in language learning: the effect of familiarity on children's repetition of four-word combinations. *Psychological Science, 19,* 241-248. Doi: 10.1111/j.1467-9280.2008.02075.x_Frequency_effects_for_multi-word_phrases/links/02e7e52e25d3999bc9000000.pdf

Boussalia, S. (2010). Students' difficulties in English-Arabic translation of collocations. Unpublished master dissertation, université des Frères Mentouri, Algeria.

Conklin, A., Schmitt, N. (2012). The processing of formulaic language. *Annual Review of Applied Linguistics, 32,* 44-61. doi: 10.1017/S0267190512000074

Darvishi, S. (2011). The investigation of collocational errors in university students' writing majoring in English. Paper presented at the 2011 International Conference on Education: Research and Innovation, Singapore. *IACSIT*. Retrieved from: www.ipedr.com

Ellis, N.C., 1996. Sequencing in SLA: phonological memory, chunking and points of order. Studies in Second Language Acquisition 18, 91±126.

Ellis, N. C., Simpson-Vlach, R., Maynard, C. (2008). Formulaic language in native and second language speakers: psycholinguistics, corpus linguistics, and TESOL. *TESOL Quarterly, 42,* 375-397. Doi:10.1002/j.15457249.2008.tb00140.x

Farrokh, P. (2012). Raising awareness of collocations in ESL/EFL classrooms. *Journal Studies in Education, 2,* 55-74. doi: 10.5296/jse.v2i3.1616

Gabrielatos, C. (1994). Collocations: Pedagogical implications, and their treatment in pedagogical materials. Unpublished essay, *Research Centre for English and Applied Linguistics,* 1-17. Retrieved from: www.academia.edu

Ganji, M. (2012). On the effect of gender and years of instruction of Iranian EFL learners' collocational competence. *English Language Teaching, (5),* 123-133. doi: 10.5539/elt.v5n2p123

Henriksen, B. Research on L2 learners' collocational competence and development –a progress report. 29-56. Retrieved from: www.eurosla.org

Kaneyasu, M. (2012). From Frequency to Formulaicity: Morphemic Bundles and Semi-Fixed Constructions in Japanese Spoken Discourse. Unpublished PhD. thesis, University of California, the United States of America.

Li, C. C. (2005). A study of collocational errors types in ESL/EFL college learners' writing. Unpublished master dissertation, Ming Chuan university, Taiwan.

Mansoor, M. S., Salman, Y. M. (2013). Collocation, colligation and semantic prosody. *Buhuth Mustaqbalia,* (43), 1-34. Retrieved from: emolex.u-grenoble3.fr

McKeown, K. R., Radev, D. R. Collocations. 1-19. New York. Retrieved from: clair.si.umich.edu

Nattinger, J.R. & DeCarrico, J.S. 1992. *Lexical phrases and language teaching.* Oxford: Oxford University Press.

Okuwaki, N. (2012). Formulaicity of language: its pervasiveness and the processing Advantage in language use. *The Tsuru university review,* 75, 1-11. Retrieved from http://trail.tsuru.ac.jp/dspace/bitstream/trair/584/1/Y075001.pdf

Perkins, M.R. 1999. Productivity and formulaicity in language development. In M. Garman, C. Letts, B. Richards, C. Schelletter & S. Edwards (eds.) *Issues in normal & disordered child language: from phonology to narrative.* Special Issue of The New Bulmershe Papers. Reading: University of Reading, 51–67.

Warren, B. (2005). A model of idiomaticity. *Proceedings of the Ninth Conference for English Studies. 35-54. Retrieved from* http://ub016045.ub.gu.se/ojs/index.php/njes/article/viewFile/270/267

Wood, D. (2009). Effects of focused instruction of formulaic sequences on fluent expression. in second language narratives: A case study12, 39-57. Retrieved   from https://journals.lib.unb.ca/index.php/CJAL/article/view/19898/21736

Wray, A. (2000). Formulaic sequences in second language teaching : principle and practice.

Wray, A. (2002). Formulaic language and the lexicon. The Pitt Building, Trumpington Street, Cambridge, United Kingdom. Cambridge University Press.

Wray, A., Perkins, M. R. (2000). The functions of formulaic language: an integrated model. *Centre for Language and Communication Research,* 20, 1-28.

CONTENTS

I want morebooks!

Buy your books fast and straightforward online - at one of world's fastest growing online book stores! Environmentally sound due to Print-on-Demand technologies.

Buy your books online at
www.morebooks.shop

Kaufen Sie Ihre Bücher schnell und unkompliziert online – auf einer der am schnellsten wachsenden Buchhandelsplattformen weltweit! Dank Print-On-Demand umwelt- und ressourcenschonend produzi ert.

Bücher schneller online kaufen
www.morebooks.shop

KS OmniScriptum Publishing
Brivibas gatve 197
LV-1039 Riga, Latvia
Telefax: +371 686 204 55

info@omniscriptum.com
www.omniscriptum.com

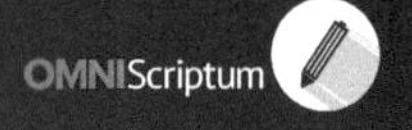

Printed by Books on Demand GmbH, Norderstedt / Germany